I0085518

Beyond Flesh

Kandice C. Mason

Edited by J. V. Stanley

Copyright © 2013 Kandice C. Mason
All rights reserved.
ISBN-13: 978-0615928418
ISBN-10: 0615928412

No part of this book may be reproduced, scanned, or distributed in any printed or electronic form, including photo copy, recording, or any information storage and retrieval system without permission of the author.

This is a work of creative fiction. Names, characters, places, and incidents either are the product of the authors' imagination, or are used fictitiously, and any resemblance to actual persons, living or dead, business establishments, or events is entirely coincidental.

Cover Design © 2013 Kandice C. Mason & J. V. Stanley
Book Design and Formatting by J. V. Stanley-Writerz Block Editing Service

To my daughter's Aeryss and Acacia.
To my mother, MaryAnn who never stopped believing.
To my sisters, De'Shawna and Coya, who showed me what it means to fight (no pun intended).
To my Dad, for encouraging my very first poem at eight-years-old.
To you. Without you, these words wouldn't come alive.

KANDICE C. MASON

CONTENTS

INTRODUCTION

Beyond Flesh goes far beyond the standard collection of poetry in that it thrusts the reader into verse imbued with passionate imagery and invigorating emotion. Kandice Mason captivates the heart and invigorates the soul with this debut collection. Using bold description, raw unabashed symbolism; she radiates the prowess of a seasoned poetess as she captivates both mind and spirit.

Through the vicious torment of heartbreak and the subtle gentle rhythm of the beauty in honest love, the musical quality of her free-form poetry will leave you swooning for more. As you hang from her every word, don't forget to breathe.

Venture into her world, beyond the monotony of underdeveloped emotion into the soul-driven passion that ignites the fire burning deep within all of us. From love, desire, and resentment; to the bitterness that threatens to consume the heart-she brings hope within the tantalizing prose. Ride along the waves with her into the bare world where emotion resides. Cast off the chains binding you to the aesthetic and embrace the beauty that exist within-the beauty that Kandice exposes in all its varying degrees.

Beyond the soul; behind your perception lies a world where pain and beauty collide. I invite you to embrace the warmth within it and take with you the eloquent embodiment of heart. Feast your eyes; within your hands lies a banquet of poetry to consume your heart and quench your spirit. Savor every word, every line, and succumb to this unfathomable world.

J. V. Stanley, Editor

CEO and Founder Writerz Block Editing Service
http://writerzblock007.wix.com/writerzblock

Author of *Fire and Water'* and *'Faces In Still Waters'*
http://jvstanley.weebly.com/

LOST MOMENTS

There are people in my life I've met fleetingly. People who I've only gotten to know by first name. People who for some reason I held back on telling them my last, as if I were afraid of them becoming close to me. This was pointless. Regardless of whether I gave them more information about me too soon, their spirit remains close to me. I think of them from time to time on sleepless nights. Rainy nights where my thoughts are muddy, but my feelings crystal clear.

Then I remember random things about you.. The way your cologne smelled, your eye color, soft, greyish, blue, and your smile with dimpled cheeks. It is then that I send you telepathic messages and I wonder if through the rain, the varying time, the fog, and the distance if you can hear me.

I would tell you: "Remember when my response was 'no'? Ask me again, and my answer would be "yes."

KEYS

I watched her, watching him.
I hated the way her eyes
danced behind thick dark lashes.
She gazed,
staring intently while
his hands glided between
white and black keys;
a sing-song melody
that only celestial bodies
could comprehend.

I look at this woman
and unbeknownst to me,
my heart opened wider than
the distance between
the sun and moon.
I envision her
as she invites herself in;
my senses heightened, aroused.
I notice the beauty mark
beneath her chin and on her left temple.
the slight pang of emotion in her eyes
as she blinks during conversation.
I memorize the cadences of her speech,
the way her eyes waltz delicately
when something from the corner catches her interest.

Today, it is the keys
that have stolen her thoughts,
those that are left unlocked.
I can see into her soul,
the way she looks intently at him
as though peering through a keyhole
that discloses the mysteries that reside
like magic within his fingertips.
She is envisioning she is the keys.

And he knows the way
To glide up,
down,

and through her
making her body sashay
to a rhythm only
they can comprehend.
He knows where to press,
where to stress
all the tight notes.
Her body no longer a body but the ocean itself,
vast and deep.
She may as well have been naked;
I have intruded into something
only meant for the privileged.

I feel as if I can catch
small glimpses of her,
taste the small remnants of her soul
despite that I don't know her, nor her soul.

The pianist stops playing
and suddenly a thought-
I think I know what will get her attention.
I make up my mind right then
to understand these mysterious black and white keys.
For they are not just the keys to understanding her...

How else could I get so intimately close?

INHALE

Inhale me deeply
into your lungs like smoke
then softly blow
me out.

I want the world to catch a whiff
through your secondhand smoke

cause I'm that powerful.
Let me be
perpetual.
Let me blow
a drift.

Sip me slowly
for I'm something worth savoring.
Not the ordinary
from the vineyards of California.
Don't gulp me; I'm worth appreciating.

Dip eagerly
into the well
of my heart.
It isn't' just water,
it's a natural resource
that you take advantage of.

FATHER'S ART

A daughter looks at her father
"Father, what is poetry?"
He replies:
"My daughter."

POEMS AND STEEL STRINGS

Mesmerizing is the
man who causes the poems to flow
from steel strings out of his hands.

Caught up in the vibrations
long after the poem is finished.
Read it, please?
Read it again,
and again…

Let me get lost in abstract thinking
and thoughts that have deeper meaning.
Let me ponder what you meant
and what your heart lets you make clear.
For that one token of a moment,
with those fingers that make poems
from steel strings.

Can I wonder
just for a second
that at one point in time
our thoughts are in sync
and that smile that plays on your lips
is there
only because you and I have shared
something deeply romantic,
and private.

Romantic because of the eloquence
That echoes through my entire being.
Romantic because of the beauty each word possesses.
Private because thoughts are only made clear
to the meticulous.
Only then can poems exist.

BREAK THE OCEAN

Must we break the ocean into infinite pieces
to discern the severity of a wrong decision
or to convey how life shattering your actions are?
If you only knew how deeply your actions portray
where your priorities lie.

Tell me,
is your reaction really consistent with the situation?
Can you admit to overreaction
or is your pride too high a flight
to come back down to earth.
Land
feet to dirt
and realize we are only human.

I see now what it is
that we can't complete a full circle
without stopping midway
or letting the line go astray.
I see now why
our emotions can sever us from other people who love us

if
we let it control us.

Why must we
cut deep into each other
the way the sheets of rain slices into the earth.
We don't have to cut
to know we have a core.

GUT INSTINCT

Let us talk about nothing,
let me just wallow.

In the breath you breathe,
swallow you whole-
I want you

to be my gut instinct.

On a rainy day
wash over me;
paint brush glide,
stroke into me.

Let the ripple effects
leave a lasting impression
in the sands of my heart.

Sit back and watch
as constellations craft
a written request of the heart.

that lack sense
to our minds

OPIUM

I want to get lost,
bend and weave chaotic patterns
and shatter all rituals…conventions.
Then stand in awe
at the massive destruction
that I have created.

I want to paint words
of places that don't match
people-obviously distorted
because I know this unnaturalness
is truth.

We are all suffering from afflictions
we keep secret.

I want to lie-
to communicate with abstract, Intellectual somersaults.
You have drowned;
you forgot to come up for air.

You cannot begin to comprehend
whether my intentions
are one-dimensional
or what it is that stirs within you.
I want to dance in circles
around you.

I don't need to take drugs
to feel opium;
I want to be drunk,
high off life
while completely cognizant
I will talk about it
as I come back down.
Walk a line not straight-
speech slurred.

Free from making sense,
free from you figuring out the combination

to my lock;
the codes,
undertones,
overtones
of my language,
and why my actions
don't quite match
my lyrical speech.

I want to be

F
   R
      E
        E

ABSTRACT SCARS

Let these abstract scars
bleed tangent
so I can see them
long enough to let them heal.
I cannot heal
what I cannot feel
with my own hand.

Recriminations
of the heart
are to prove
love is an
abstract perception
that only exists
separately.

An individual truth,
fingerprint-
never the same curve, line, or groove

but yet-
it was you that asked me
why my butterflies were wet
and whether or not you could
taste them.

Coward!
For making me fall so deeply
inside of you
then not allowing me
the key
to get back out again.

MEN IN MY LIFE

Multilateral
prismatic in the faces they show.
Phase in and out,
in and out,
in and out
of my life
like the moon-

a reel,
silent film,
flickering.

Concrete
until the lights come back on,
then dimming.

STRIP

"You want me to strip?"
while you gaze hungrily
at my mahogany skin.

Nipples erect
bulge elevated,
you drink
liquor from
perfumed breasts.

Close is not
close enough
when wanting to devour
someone whole.

I tease
tongue pirouettes
around your neck and ear.

I unveil

and whisper:

"Strip for me.
Let me gaze hungrily
at the inner workings
of a seemingly shallow
tenebrous flesh."

Who believes
my body is no temple
or gold.

Collecting remnants
of another lost, dismembered
moonless soul.

HOW SKELETONS FORM

A sentence
began as a thought.
Your words unravel
in a thick spiral
before me
springing to life.

I am amazed at their capabilities-
to fabricate truth
equipped with embellishments
that would make a telepath
tilt their head to one side.

We are all guilty of playing
a game of chess
protecting our fragile inner selves
from the perceived callousness
of others.

Bored with our prosaic lives,
we keep inventing
rich tapestries
of illusion;
afraid of banal existence,
afraid to die,
and become reborn.

Do we realize this self-inflicted paralysis?

Often our collisions
with others
fuse an oscillation
inside us
that would allow growth

yet we hide
behind infinite images-
portrayals of who we wish to
condemn…
Ourselves,

Others...
to only know
partial truths
complete with whole lies.

This is where broken marriages
step in
while distraught fathers step out.
Women seek the warmth
of a man twice her age
and a preteen drags
her first breath of a cigarette.
The artwork of our hurt-
a result
of agile thoughts
capitulating
to perverseness.

KANDICE C. MASON

HOPSCOTCH

Children play hopscotch
on crippled concrete
near a cemetery;
death frame,
sidewalk chalk,
life and lifeless-
juxtaposed.

Living and dying poem-
montage
to ponder over.

Cemented world
swallowing non-asphalt life.
Their laughter risen
then it too,
dies.

I DIDN'T KNOW IT

I didn't know it but
I was walking on eggshells when I fell
for you.
With every step,
my surface cracked
beneath me
as I tried to reach my destination.
See my future
with glassy eyes,
but glass breaks
when melting hearts
collided with slippery flesh.
We created life bonds
that came with 163 heartbeats;
a physical manifestation
growing beautiful
because we couldn't.
Truth is,
I fall in love with your face every day
because you are in her.
No matter the sad words exchanged,
how much the glass continues
to break,
or the eggshells that crack beneath me-
I know that although I'm spinning,
my world completely stops
when I watch our love grow.

SSSSSHHHHHH

I can feel my pulse beating in my fingertips
and taste the faint flavor of loneliness with every sip
of this life I'm drinking.
It leaves a bittersweet aftertaste,
but I'm too tired to wash it out,
or maybe I just don't know how.

In the night my body hums
a melancholy song only sad people know and hear,
waiting for him to put his finger to mouth
'Ssshhhhhhh, no more humming.
I'm here,
I'm here."

With each ache,
with each drop poured from cheeks
damp for too many nights,
the clock ticks
and I resist
impulses to settle
for less than perfect.

WHEN WINTERS ARE FRIGID

When winters are frigid,
bodies call names in whispers,
then screams
begging for human blankets
that burst at the seams
from overuse.
It's never too much
and that hot chocolate warms
but it also cools-
the burning sensation
of yearning;
cups of artificial warmth
wrapped snug in
coffee mugs.

For some
soft notes
of wind chills,
carry the night
in its cradle-
ringing in the ears
bitten hard by
rough wintery kisses-
love bites.

The moon drips,
staining the pillow skies
with silver pepper.
Sleep knocks softly-
tomorrow pounds hard.

HOW FRUIT TASTES

Let this fruit spill
just enough to fill
every crevice of your being
with nectar
from something that was
just being
alive,
because we aren't the only ones living.

Maybe the sweet
will magically pour into you
and the day you meet me,
your body will weep
letting sweetness seep
into me.

Those bottomless
secrets
that exist within me
will dissolve into certainty
that I share with you.
My intensity doesn't frighten;
you're honest, too.

You can see the way that I see you,
watch me continue living
in you.

I search for an extension of myself
that I never knew existed;
loving who I am
because of who I am with you.
I realized how sweet
fruit is,
the day that I met you.

TEXTURED THOUGHTS

During a conversation
he told me I had
textured thoughts
that produce
textured words.
It would take
a sensitive soul
to truly feel them.
To others,
I make no sense-
just fragmented sentences
with no complete
perception
of what I want to convey.
It's exhilarating
to wrap, coil, and enchain
my words
around yours.
Let them embrace…
I love the way
your words taste
draped against mine
with delicate undertones
of sweetness
upon every breath.

KANDICE C. MASON

NO STARS

Opening the door,
she walks out,
brings a cigarette
to her lips
and watches the smoke
infiltrate the air above her.

It's late,
night blankets us-
clings to us
despite
that we're barely covered.

Lace and heels
cause men to honk their horns
loudly, and others
to stop dead
just to say
a sultry 'Hello'.
They try to disguise the real reason
for such a generic greeting.

"No stars…" she says.
"Oh, it's probably because
of all the lights," I reply.
"No." she responds, definitively.
"It's because of this place…"

I look up again,
reflecting upon her words.

This street,

this moment,

our lives-

cars drive by swiftly
as if trying to escape
the way the stars have.

MY MUG

I remember when I first met you
I had asked if I could hold your hand
and it didn't register,
not then,
that I wouldn't or couldn't
let go

of what was
and what had been;
I couldn't see past
the night, my dreams.

Despite the reality of my
daydreams
as they play out realistically in my mind,
they feel wrong.

Emotional punches
hit hard;
my physical body
believes it can take it,
but my mind won't forget.

You and I,
we aren't perfect;
we're so different.
How could I not expect
that at some point in time
your world would crash into mine?
That your truth
would be my lie?

Your body
pours freely
into any cup,
while mine
merely falls
into my favorite mug.

DAYS FILLED

Days filled with
apple trees,
pear trees,
pineapple,
grape vines,
natural aloe vera,
cactus,
clovers,
kisses,
fingers lacing,
sugared words,
warm touches.

Days filled with
lost thoughts,
only for a warm friend
to find them.

Days filled with
the sound of my laughter,
and I haven't heard it
in a while
but it sounds beautiful.
And he says I'm the
delicate flavor of wine-
and that is beautiful

LOST PAINTING

Watching these colors drift,
blend over and under
a mesh.

Dull, beige,
Soft almonds,
Lovely chestnut browns…

I guess this is
what making love looks like.
I guess this is where
one-night stands
up
on her heels,
to give the day a kiss,
while stars swing
in sky parks
making love.

Making…
beer-tinged kisses,
coy smiles
mixing
warm breath,
sliding fingers
and slippery flesh
on stained sheets.

Another lost painting
embedded with more than color,
more than the infusion of harmonious tones-
saturated with emotion.

SHIFTING

Swaying pendulum,
you unfold before me
like wings
opening for a moment,
then closing.
Shy leaves peaking,
swinging door;
pendulum in my heart
excruciatingly incapable
of remaining stationary
long enough to fathom
with complete certainty
how much you really mean to me.

Motion,
rhythm,
heartbeat
enclosed in
water

with uncertain waves
of pleasure and pain
that crash to the shore
of my mind.

THESE WORDS

These words I hear
splatter the walls inside my head,
and on broken days
a broken record persists-
clawing away at
broken thoughts and
laughing away at broken hearts.
They try to mend themselves
with a broken needle.

How does it feel to lose yourself
within yourself
while simultaneously,
get lost in something else?
No, I say;
I'd rather be able to find myself

But these words they say
pour down
through a silken haze;
opaque vapor
causing decay.
Why do you let this get to you,
the stuff that people say?

Receptive spirits consume all energies,
even the ones with ill motive at play.

CALLOUSED HANDS

Is it true
that calloused hands
are the holders of callous hearts?
That each perpetual line emblazoned on fingertips
hold the secrets?
The depth of your flesh
proving you're more than just skin deep.

Or is my imagination running away with me,
taking depth to a more shallow region
as I try to conceptualize
your actions,
and why the stars have fallen out of the sky.
Yet again,
in my world,

I try to interpret why it is
that callousness is commonplace
and an acceptable form of communication
in response to your incessant fuck-ups.

SNOW GLOBES

Snow globes exist on earth
in the depths of lovers hearts-
drifting flakes on drunken souls
caught in a whirlwind
limited emotion
tunnel vision
masochistic prison
yet touch, no restriction.

Bodies speak
when words do not
and yours are drums
until I hum,
but we aren't really conversing,
are we?

And I just lay there
my expression downcast
on thoughts
of a threaded silk pillow-
a fabricated nothing
with built-in lies.
Truths weaved within,
embedded in you
in bed with you.

DESCRIBE MISSING YOU

Shuttering

Loneliness

Every hour

Every day

Pain

Inconsolable

Night

Grief

UNZIPPED

She unzipped herself today.
Inside
stairs ascended and descended,
puddles of bottomless water
existed.

Fractured elevators
lurked behind
jeweled doors
laced with tear drops
that made you think
those diamonds lead
to greater beauty.
No, not at all,
Just more destruction.

She unbuttoned the top
of her mind's dress,
removed the silk panties
that she usually
kept in a drawer
of her eyelids.
Without further
Introspection,
I popped the top
off those lids,
a spider
seeped through the crack.

With further assessment,
I knew that I couldn't
go further
without researching
scientific explanations
for the absurdity
of her chaos.

It simply isn't right
to delve into
uncharted territory.

CAN YOU HELP ME PUT THIS ON?

I turn around
with my back facing him.

He gently scoops my hair
from the back of my neck,
and then lifts it.
His touch
gives me butterflies.

I laugh
'I'll hold my hair' I say.

I hand him the necklace
take hold of my hair.

His pelvis presses against me,
molds into me,
but he is not mine.

CURRENT

Can you see it?
The current that exists between them-
delicate as a water color,
subtle as a ray.

No words spoken;
bodies hold a language
only lovers understand.

Eyes talk,
hands speak-
you brush past,

converse with me?

INTENSITY

You said the intensity was too much,
that my stare was not fair-
it had penetrated your defenses
suddenly and unexpected.

Somewhere in your warped mind-
'deep' is for shallow people
which is why you tread
those superficial waters.

Love is for fools
and you'd rather be smart.

A challenge is for cretin's
and thinking is only skin deep.

You prefer the black and white
over the detestable grey area.
'Keep it cut and dry' you'd say.

You'd rather replace complexity
with beautiful simplicity-
intricacy is for losers;
fallacies are far more interesting than truth.

You'd rather I not be your truth.

TRUTHS

I had the chance to learn your truths today.
You exposed them to me

the way the moon exposes
life inside darkness.

Yes, the sky may still cry
puddles as big as oceans
and the length of rivers,

but life remains in this world of madness.
Roses bloom while everyone sleeps;
roses still bloom
when people are in mourning.

QUESTION MARK

There was a time
when I sought nurturance from you
the way a baby would seek
a mother's breast.
You filled me,
I grew,
and I was whole.

You said you couldn't let me go
but south to demolish
everything that made me stay.

Perhaps the distance that now separates us
will allow a new foundation to uphold us-
to fortify what had crumbled,
to renew what aged
when our love decayed.

How did we get to the point
where what made us a sentence,
no longer has a period?
Every time we speak,
our devotion ends with a question mark?

FADE

Sometimes the way things play out in your mind
doesn't match the way events play out in life.
Your mind is left to reconstruct
but sometimes you're not strong enough
and thus begin to deconstruct.

How is it that my body can live without my mind?
I can feel myself walking
Without knowing where I'm going.
I feel myself breathing
but don't feel as if I'm living.
As I write these words, my thoughts-
fade
in and out like a dying heartbeat.

I'm digging in my pockets,
searching to find
what once was mine,
but I'm coming up empty.
I guess I need to stop searching through pockets
in search of a heart.

HERE WE LAY

Like a broken melody,
trembling staccato
on an inharmonious night,

I wrote 'I love you' in your hand
while you were sleeping.
When morning came,
it washed away.

Once again, you utter words
of sincere apology
that are incongruous with your actions.
If my shoes are your feet
and in your hands my spirit,
why is our love so fragmented?
Fickle, like the weather,
I beg of you-
reassemble my heart.

ROSES TO DUST

I never knew
I'd have to mix tears and blood
or that one day these tears might flood
and drown me.
I'd recover only
to realize that I've been treading
upon water pouring from my eyes.
I didn't realize
I carried so much within me.

Surprisingly, I'm not bitter,
just a little warped.
My mind has a few loose screws-
nothing that can't be fixed
but just enough to make me sick.

You wonder why it is
that I don't raise a fist
when you call me a bitch.
You say when I was 16, I knocked the shit out of you
when you called Me out my name.
What happened to that girl?
She got burned in flames.

You say I lost my fire,
you think it went up in flames
but I'm still fuming.
I shouldn't be mad
because you made me feel as though I'm nothing.

My name is synonymous with the name 'whore'
and you lost count, so I began to invent more
people who can fill the hole that has burnt deep
and no one knows I'm the holder of secrets-
or the sadness I keep.

WHEN SLEEP NEVER COMES

Those nights when I can't fall asleep,
when I toss and turn in my bed,
when my eyes close by my mind does not,
I call you at 2:21 a.m.
You're groggy from sleep
but you sacrifice the sweet void of sleep
and dedicate your attention to me.

The deep even tone of your voice
plants a small seed of calmness
that washes over my mind,
putting me into the most peaceful state.

For once I can feel
my body become less tense.
I can feel my own voice soften,
my breath rhythmic and slow.
I can feel sleep creeping around the corners
with the gentle lull of your voice.

I can sleep
when my thoughts can lay inside yours.
'Goodnight, my baby,' you say
but I had already risen from the prison of consciousness
and fallen asleep.

CUPID'S WHISPER

Cupid whispered in my ear,
drew me in
as I felt myself gasp in the ecstasy of his sweet words.
He awakened me
and let you breathe life
into me
the day I met you.

You breathed life into me
the way the wind blows air into the water
creating the ocean's breeze.
The way the moon
breathes onto the earth,
illuminates what the naked eye couldn't see.

I sucked it in, rejoiced in cupid's melody.
I needed the fresh scent in my lungs.
It seeped through me
invading my nostrils,
ravished me;
encircled me in its arms.

Cupid whispered in my ear today,
caressed me with his tantalizing imagery-
laced me in his mystery.
His hypnotic whispers,
forced me
to allow you to be
the siren in my ear.

MY DEFINITION

I was young at a time
but not too young to see
how in love I thought you guys were.

Mom and Dad
sneaking kisses
thinking
no one was watching.

Family gossip leaking,
learning that the both of you had
spent every waking moment
with each other
when you were my age.
'So young…' they'd say.
Surely what you felt was real!

Afraid
to admit that I want someone,
need someone.
Don't think
I can ever let anyone
into the diary of my life.
Mom and Dad,
you two were my definition;
I thought at one time
definitions were truth.

Kissing
both of you
at separate times,
each declaring how much you love
the knots that tie you together.
Why can't we be the knot
that kept you loving each other?

IF I COULD HAVE ONE WISH

I wish I could get inside your head
and learn about how you think,
then I wouldn't make you so angry-
wouldn't feel like I have to peek
behind a curtain into your thoughts.
You would readily share them with me
and I would be happy
knowing you could trust me with such precious ideas.
Trust me, I believe in them
and I cherish everything you think, say, or feel.
You are a part of me
as I am of you.

WHAT YOU SAY

You say you can show me the world,
all the places I never knew
and I don't hesitate to fall.
I fall hard
because of the romantic part of me.
Nobody said
I would eventually hit the floor,
my heart a liquid crimson
pool of love
I drown within.
I think I fell too hard.

CLASSIC

You can watch me grow and change,
watch me grow old.
I'm like that old school jam you play on your stereo,
I'm like that memory you can't get out of your head.
I may get old as will you,
but I'll always be-
an ageless beauty
lasting, eternal.
Much like a fine wine,
I only get better through the passage of time.
I'm a classic, baby.

LOVERS TALK THAT TALK

Lovers always talk
of giving their hearts away,
surrendering to some unknown-
a feeling that can't ever be described accurately.

We don't give our hearts away-
at least I didn't.
It was stolen;
I kind of wish I had kept it for myself.

Don't know
if this unreal nothing
actually is a concrete something.
All I know
is what I can hear, touch, taste, smell,
and see.

Lovers think they know so much,
but when they die
the only thing they will have left
are the memories-
collaborations of senses.
It is in everything.

All I
hear,
touch,
taste,
smell,
and see-

your love all of this to me.

CALENDAR MOURNING

I remember,
but the world keeps trying to forget
everything about you that I miss.

In January,
the hours went by
one-o-clock
two-o-clock;
what have I done?

February came
bringing with it the wind.
How I wished it swept you back to me
but only shivers it did send.

March came and went
stomping through like a cavalry.
I wrote and wrote blank pages
of nothingness and cried

April came and
I thought I saw you in my room;
such a surreal illusion.
How can an ethereal feeling
result in sad confusion.

May brought sunshine
and warmth from the sky.
Too bad it didn't extend to my heart;
the world has forgotten
about you and I

The sun still rose,
the night still fell,
the flowers still bloomed;
but June filled my heart with gloom.

Clear blue waters
Fresh, naked sky...
Why don't the stars cry out from the sky?

July seems dull without you by my side.

I knew the summer was ending,
when August came.
I miss the burning desire I felt
when you first uttered my name.

September brings with it
the anniversary of my birth.
Usually I'm fine
but it's the first time without you,
the flush in my cheeks fades to a desolate hue.

October was scary
because it reminded me
that I have no one to hold
when something frightens me.

Family came on a November day
and for once I was not upset-
for once I was okay, but
with the evening moonlight my sadness crept
and wouldn't go away.

In December I thought
about the years that have past,
same ol' same-
time seems to go fast.

Why doesn't the world stand still for you-
stop spinning and acknowledge you too?
The seasons should cease,
the world should stop;
the stars should cry out of the sky.
Why can't the world stand still
if just for a moment,
bow its head
give a moment of silence.

In January
the hours went by...
one-o-clock
two-o-clock,

BEYOND FLESH

what have I done?
Absolutely nothing;
blank pages have won.

I KNOW WHERE YOUR SECRETS LIE

Behind that mask of many years-
dig deeper,
dig deeper,
not so discreet
when written on paper...
I know where your secrets lie.

I cannot fathom,
nor can understand-
secrets are like rocks.
Those rocks turn into boulders,
boulders to volcanoes
whose sharp edges leave
big gashes in the heart.

Secrets are like turbulent waters
turned to ice
accumulating into a glacier
that unravels into an avalanche.
I know where your secrets lie,
behind those grey eyes-
breaking loving ties.

A THOUSAND YEARS

Sometimes I feel like I've cried a century-
a thousand years,
with enough tears to fill an ocean.
If my tears were filled in buckets,
there would be enough to replenish the waters
of the Aral sea.

KANDICE C. MASON

KISSING MY HANDS

Tonight, I kissed my own hands;
I wanted to take away the hole that consumed me.
The emptiness of this bedroom-
it is so lonely without you.
Tell me how it is,
tell me how it is,
that I am to console myself
as tears flow from my cheeks,
puddles on my pillow.
It's a lonely night without you,
As you lay on the couch.

UNIVERSALLY UNDERSTOOD

The more my heart listens to the sound of the world,
the more I wonder what it is my own heart is missing.
I wonder what it is that stirs so deep within me,
why I respond so profoundly;
to voices of others, music, journals, art, and words.

I then begin to wonder if I can tap into others
the way they tap into me.
Could it be?
They really feel me,
respond to
all of my hopes, every dream, every glance, every breath;
every downpour of emotions.
Could it be?
They respond to me;
they really feel me.

Are people as perceptive
as I hope them to be?
Can every emotion felt by living things
be interpreted into any language,
transcribed into something universally understood?
Could it be,
          could it be,
                    could it be
responding to me?
Am I as close to you
as you are to me?

OUR SOULS

Tonight is just that-
a night
where my soul has awakened
for another day
to mingle with yours.

'Penny for your thoughts'
my soul says to yours-
but you shut your book,
lock it with a key;
you say your thoughts are only meant for me.

You say other souls cannot be trusted-
your soul is not worth the beauty of mine.
'Well then, ante up a dime,' I replied,
because your thoughts are more precious
than all things divine.

I say I will fight for your key,
open your book,
read all of your soul.

To which you protested, saying I mustn't,
begged me, *'Please, don't touch it!'*
You thought that I couldn't handle the real you,
Your inadequacies, inconsistencies.

'My dear soul,' I say.
I was sure your thoughts bloomed as flowers.
I dreamed to lace your thoughts in my heart,
along with the inadequacies,
each and every inconsistency-
painting with artistic beauty
with a lack of pattern that provides stimulating intricacy.
Won't you please share your thoughts with me?

Slowly, cautiously, you open your book
and read from it.
I listened intently, my mind a flood of images-

overwhelmed with all that you've shown me.
You were right all along,
there were just some things that I simply didn't understand-
others, I feared.
The more your mind's eye spoke
the more my ears fixated upon your words.
Even so, I still wanted all of you.

You sensed my fear, however;
and swiftly closed the book,
not quite ready for what I held sacred.
Perhaps another time I will show you more, you say.
More when I'm ready, I say.

AROUSE

Arouse
this right here,
this very spot
right now.
Like that,
don't stop.
I'm just about to…
explode
with all the love you bring me.

Caress
right here,
like that.
Stay close,
I want to hear
you
say it…
Exactly!
I love you too.

Just don't,
not now.
Say you won't,
not ever
stop loving me.
Pretend
this night,
all nights,
have no end.
I want to erase where you end
and I begin.

IN THE NIGHT

In the night
something whispers
in disguise,
wrapped around the veil
of the night stars.

Something lurks,
creeping ever so silent
into doors left ajar.
Seeping through the cracks

as you lay in your most vulnerable state;
they creep in next to you
while you try to sleep,
waiting,
to get that piece of you.

All that is kind,
Spirited, and free-
All that lies good within me,
yours to take.
You are
cruelty, envy, hatred, jealousy, and inadequacy
bound tight.
You are the reason
for sleepless nights.

LET NOT

Let not emotions cut deep
like swords into the mouths of hearts.
Let not my heart be overcome with consumption,
as alcohol the intoxication.

If there not be a single uttered word
that is concerned with compassion,
let not it pass
or seek redemption;
for ill words left lingering
is earth shattering.

Can you not
do that thing you do;
the coldness of your mind
pierces my heart
because you utter the remains
of what lies within it.
Soon thereafter,
you ask me to forget it,
but that is not fair.

Positivity slips through your fingers
like that of a fish,
while negativity clutches your throat-

how I wish I could slit it.

INERTIA

There is a pulse that beats within me
so remarkably fast, it sounds like a hum.
It is this pulse that drives me to do
the forbidden.

As long as this hum persists,
why should my body resist
the temptation to be perpetually raw and natural?

I cultivate my life according to a set of rules;
these rules beget limitations and boundaries
that I do not permit myself to cross
until I dream.

Perhaps this means
I'm more truthful
when I'm asleep...
Laws are for the weak
unable to take that leap

into the immeasurable vacancy.
Does this make me deep?
Caught between heaven and hell;
my earth, my life,
void.

TRICKS

The crescent moon
bleeds silver,
pricks its finger
onto the inky night sky,

and then dips its bleeding light
onto this sheet of paper-
illuminating my thoughts
into clarity.
When people read it,
they feel me.

Crescent turns to full,
playing tricks with my mind.
The more light that bleeds,
the more my mind's eye sees
and if I see before I'm ready,
then the moon is full of deceit.

Into my dreams I drift-
to others, I sleep angelic,
however, inside
a storm persist
prisoner to an incubus
preying on the negativity
that eats at me while conscious.

TRANSITIONING

I'm used to looking at everything
with a critical eye-
but as time propels forward,
I'm allowing myself to take a step back
allowing your love to take a step in.

I see the skeptics
and the way they look at
the choices we made.

They think that holding their breath
disguises their disbelief-
but I'm no fool...
I have a gift for reading others
and my eye, it sees many fallacies
in my inner-self as well as within others.

But one thing these others can't fault us on
is trying
because we could just let
it fall.
To fall would be to fail
and that could never be.

What we are doing
is growing, maturing,
and transitioning
into the people we know we can be-
for ourselves, and the other
growing inside me.

LEILANI

Petals dance underneath fingertips
when I first felt your flesh.
Fragile and fresh from the heavens;
you are my celestial flower,
delicate, sweet baby.

Your eyes may not see
and your thoughts
may seem incomprehensible to me
are probably more deep
than I could ever fathom them to be.
163
is the number of times in which your heart beats
for me, for me.

When I held you inside,
I learned what it was to have two souls present.
Four lungs to breathe,
Four eyes to see-
so new to me
and full of new meanings.
My heaven, my earth,
My miracle-
your birth

SWEPT AWAY

When I first met you, I thought I could gaze into your soul
and I wasn't afraid to show that I had been searching
behind the closed doors of your lids
waiting for you to finish blinking so I could gaze again.
I thought I knew you,
the very depth of you.
But I've realized naiveté flexes its arms
when I'm around you.
The eyes can be deceiving sometimes
especially those who master the art.
I fell into you behind closed doors
quietly and instantly
and couldn't find my way back out again.
There are nights when I watched you while you slept
while wondering about that name
that stumbled from your lips.
Your heart pours out the truth
foreign to me.
The name,
but not the gender.
I wander around sleepless
wondering why I keep relinquishing my treasures to you
when you've bequeathed them
to someone else.

SURREAL

I sat inside your love today
and your spirit's rays caught mine.
I think I've met you somewhere before
Maybe in a past life?
I think I've fallen for you
many times before.
Serendipity?
I've never felt so safe
knowing there's no escape
as I linger in your translucent glow.
It's like
your touch sends telepathic lightning though me;
its passion flows through my body and trickles down to my fingertips.
The tears subside
and for once I can feel free and alive-
reborn.
I can feel your electric pulse inside of me
and I savor it.

SO READY

Getting tired of being lonely-
ready to taste love again.
Let it linger on my tongue-
marinate in my mouth.
Drink it all in
allowing it to drip down my chin,
an excuse to have you lick it off.

Getting tired of being lonely-
ready to surrender
Like dust to the wind
Gravity to earth
Butterflies to nectar
Fish to water
Your hair to the breeze
I'm down
on my knees

Ready to surrender
Like a body does
To a tantalizing whisper

Getting tired of being lonely-
ready to fall and keep falling
off the highest mountain.
Hell, out of the sky!
And know that through it all,
after years of falling
that you had decided to wait
through the time that has elapsed in my existence

to catch me.

READ ME

If you could...
I wish you would
open me up,
read me
because I'm not the mystery
you think me to be.

If you would indulge
in the folds
the crevices of my being,
you will see what is written
is something worth thinking
over,
and over again.
I'm not simple
but I trust you to comprehend.

I want to share my wonders;
my lakes, rivers, and water it
            f
         a
           l
           l
            s.

My mountains, valleys
are exactly what made me a water lily
surviving through the muck
that always seems to fuck
our lives up.
I want you to be a part of it,
of me.

I want to show you how words can b r e a k,
how words can
F
  A
    L
      L

      U
Get back P
again.
I want to show you who
and what I am.

MIRROR IMAGE

Summer nights,
clammy hands-
I am nervous to hold your hand.
I tentatively expose the lines of my palm
as you do with an intensity that rivals my own.
Trust is the guiding light that far outshines the light of

the fireflies that light up at twilight.
Sweet kisses embellish skin
as we lay on the moist grass together.
Strands of hair, you gently tug,
I turn, and kiss your fingertips.

Your eyes are my eyes tonight,
my hand is your hand,
and my heart beats in a syncopated rhythm with yours.

Our thoughts are a mirror image tonight
and I am locked within the beauty of it all,
the vanity.
In love with my reflection
that reflects you.
In love with my mirror,
my mirror, you.

OVERFLOW

You see?
Over there?
Beyond the forest lies
a point in time

where I inhaled too much
and the glass became full.
So my ideas poured over
and the words spilled over
onto these sheets of paper.

The thoughts kept forming,
my mind kept replenishing
with more and more to share.
So I have no choice;
when there is abundance,
I must share.
I have to convey
my innermost thoughts
to you.

NEVER THOUGHT

Never thought I'd meet someone like you.
Someone who makes me examine my soul,
makes me think twice about my words;
makes me delve deeper into the convolutions of my mind.
Someone who makes me want to beautify myself
from the inside out.

Take out all the negative
and replace with things more positive
because I know that you're looking at my soul
and not my flesh.

Never thought I'd ever meet someone like you.
Someone that carries themselves with such gracefulness,
with the stance of a king.
Someone who makes me value everything I have to offer
and makes me want to hide my temper.

Hide my thoughts behind a curtain,
don't think they can be as profound as yours.
I don't know if the windows to my soul are beautiful enough
or if the scenery I provide would impress
the intricate design of your mind.
I would love to make love to you,
mentally, that is.

So I could experience what it's like to be one
with someone that impresses my mind,
moves my heart,
and lightens my spirit.
No, I've never met anyone quite like you.

INDEFINITE FLAME

My heart is an infinite flame.
It burns and coils with everything I have ever felt.
Alive and true with so many chambers, secrets, desires, and thoughts.
It has a mind of its own.

Everything I have ever thought, witnessed or experienced
is inscribed permanently into my heart
before transitioning into my brain.
Those memories then make their way into my mouth
where I cannot possibly reiterate everything my heart has told me
with as much proficiency.
Continuing on into my eyes
show cased for the world to see
causing tears to seep into puddles
onto my cheeks.

Everything I have ever felt;
all my secrets, desires, and thoughts
are an indefinite flame.
Running eternally; each in correspondence with the other
creating a chain effect.
I wish my eyes weren't such a tattle-teller
and I could fool everyone into believing their vacancy.

BRIMMING

A new day is brimming
on the surface off the coast
of the ocean.
My undoing is a scent within the air
where I can be free…

…and I'm liking it.
I'm tearing down brick walls
paying close attention to the sound of nature;
The birds as they keep leaving songs
on my doorstep.
They wait patiently
for me to open the envelope,
waiting for the sound of my heart.
Leaning in close, they listen to what
romance sounds like
and these emotions wrapped around me
like the rustle of feathers
warming my soul with their down.

I no longer have to pry
into depth to feel deep
or have another cold night
of sleep
because everything has just begun
chirping.
It's beginning to look a lot like spring.
I'm ready for all the romantic flings
and getting' excited over the little things.

Smiles and laughter,
gay ass poems like this.
Damn, the way you kiss
makes my heart flutter,
my mind wonder
my belly

f
l
i
p
 f
l
o
p

I'm undone
but it's okay that the world is spinning.
It means I'm alive-
that this is only just the beginning
and everything is brimming over the surface.

JUST LAYING HERE

And I'm just layin' here
up this late at night.
Just want to paint this picture
that I see in my mind.
Maybe get it transcribed-
put it in a notebook,
make it come alive.

Because I can just see it;
just picture it,
you and me.
We can do this
but I'm not really a romantic.

I'm just a little passionate
and wanna be a little less lonely tonight.
So I'm going to kiss you
even though we aren't official
because it just feels right.

And the night is officially young
because it's like two in the morning
and this relationship is officially young
because it has just began blooming.

But I can just picture it,
had to get it inscribed
so I have proof that it is legitimate.

And I don't wanna pretend,
nor do I want you to be fictitious
if you're not feelin' it.

Just hoping for once my mind agrees with your body,
and my body agrees with your mind.
Because I need somebody
and yeah, like I said, I can picture it.

A LUXURY

I traveled a long way to meet you;
long before I first inhaled.
I had built a map
on a quest to search for you

and I traversed
across waters
and over mountains.
Roamed countries
just to walk in step with you,
breathe the air you breathe,
see the things you see.

I followed the scent of your aura,
traced the remnants of your soul.
I built traps to ensnare you,
Although, they weren't really traps.
I relied on my laugh,
my intellect,
my *passion*
to satiate you.
If I could speak another language
I'd speak a thousand different ways
of how much I wanted to know you.

And then as chance would have it,
I found you.
You knew from that moment
I wanted to keep you.
So I didn't hesitate to ask
if I could.

"I don't understand
why you love me.
I'm not rare or exceptional."
you'd say,
but it's not meant to be understood.
Love is like that-its unusual.
Your ordinary is my extraordinary.

You make me believe in fantasy.

"I don't understand
why you need me."
I don't need you.
Needs are necessities
and you, my dear, are a luxury.

Yet, you still weren't sure.
You broke my heart
and I set you free.
But then you traveled the distance
and ventured back.

I don't know why you came back;
I thought you didn't need me.
But then you said:

"Needs are necessities
and you, my darling, I've come to realize
are my luxury.
A luxury I'll spend a lifetime paying for
if need be."

EL ALMANECER

Sunrise
awoke transition
into a new day;
a new life.
So I tried to cultivate my thoughts
to accommodate growth and regeneration.

As my thoughts continued to propagate
along with the growth inside me,
I had decided to grasp at the tendrils of thought
inside
to find a therapeutic cleansing.

I inhale this new life;
I bring forth new life
Through the very air that I breathe.
I can only hope
That the experience will be refreshing,
stimulating,
but above all
invigorating.

Eager for my inner child to take a step back,
my mature adult steps
into the realm that surpasses expectations
and makes a path for new generations.

I pray that higher knowledge holds me in its embrace.
I pray that I will always receive a loving, helping hand
and continue to overcome
the obstacles that lay before me.
I want to make God proud that he made me.

FLESH

Soon I will die-
spread me across the ocean
so I may for once be a partial remnant
of something beautiful
because I couldn't quite get it right
in this life.

Tell me again
why I captured your heart,
touched your fingertips,
and caressing memories
so deep
it
hit the shore.

Tip your hat,
let your hand extend down
to lift
and kiss mine.

Let all words I have ever spoken
float down-
forever embedded
in your heart.

SHOOTING STAR

Seeing this shooting star
felt as if the universe
winked
our little secret
then smiled
it's confidentiality
into the wind.
For me to feel.
For me to feel real-
validated

Similar to...

Meeting you in flesh.
The gasp.
The butterflies.

Your introduction
into my life
just as Poetic
as your departure,
although that part
long gone
still holds
depth
deeper than logic
could convey

because death
death in word, spirit, body mind
is only
the beginning.

This shooting star
makes me remember
the way you
made my strawberries run lush
under a September night

when your eyes tasted of magic
and your skin saw innocence
transform
into a woman.

SOUL MATE

I think I've known you many lifetimes; in different forms, styles, manners Although the point in which I fell in love with you may have varied every time, the amount of love I had for you never did. In those lifetimes, we may not have always been together, but the impact you carried on my life was life-altering. I'm always learning from you. In each time of life you give me lessons I could never teach myself.

RESURFACE

$\mathcal{S}$ometimes, it is as if she looks at me and every vicious remark, every action meant to harm, every second I made to hurt, she comes rushing toward me, a tsunami - I cannot erase. That is why I've given up. That is why I look away. If I truly were sorry, which I am, who can live with that sort of guilt on a daily basis? Who can walk past someone knowing they are the cause for unforgivable, insurmountable amounts of pain that is liable to resurface at any given moment?

FALLING

I always thought
the time it takes a leaf to fall
to the ground
is how long it takes
to fall in love.

I think I gazed at my daughter
for that length of time.

Been contemplating
that night we made love
and just before your release
you kindly asked if I were ready
to receive it.

And I remember
between ins and outs
I love you escaped
from your lips.
Me, being so shocked
by the sincerity,
almost forgetting to respond

I just keep flipping these instances
like a coin
trying to decide
what time I really fell

and it bothers me
I still don't know.

CHILD-LIKE

I run-
he chases,
bringing out the child in me,
bringing out the magic in me.
I know longer 8
but somewhere near a quarter.

Hiding in the shades of tree's;
him saying the way the light
hits my hair and eyes
makes me beautiful as the sky
is heavenly
and I
shaking my head
at him comparing me.

The skies allure-
the clouds,
the leaves...
I'm not a celestial body;
I'm somewhere in between heaven
and the sea.

He just so happened to catch a glimpse of
the interminable
side of me.

SWEET DREAMS

And I want you to know
that when this life's a nightmare,
you're sweet dreams-
And I want sweet dreams every night.

And I want you to know
waking up to you
is sunrise -
and I want to see the sunrise
every morning.

And I want you to know
that blending days and nights
is life
and
you are my days,
you are my nights.

KANDICE C. MASON

BEYOND FLESH

KANDICE C. MASON

Kandice Mason lives with her two children in a small town in North Carolina. She received a B.A in English with a minor in creative writing from the University of North Carolina at Pembroke. This is her first published book of poetry. She enjoys baking, outdoors, reading, and traveling.

She enjoys feedback from her readers and would greatly enjoy hearing from you. She can be found at
http://www.facebook.com/people/Kandice-Celeste-Mason/55763227

For updates on her writing, be sure to like her official Facebook page.

https://m.facebook.com/fleshtofleshbyKandiceCelesteMason?id=5786813
62169244&_rdr

BEYOND FLESH

KANDICE C. MASON

www.ingramcontent.com/pod-product-compliance
Lightning Source LLC
Chambersburg PA
CBHW060951040426

42445CB00011B/1100